Cuddle Puddle

Wholesome poems

by
Michael Cox

GW00385097

ISBN: 9798693698963
Imprint: Independently published

To Frankie, for keeping us all together and assuring us that everything's going to be ok.

Contents

Entwined

We met under the flicker of a thousand fairy glows.
Music weaving it's magic into us, crafting how this spell
will go.

Glimpses caught from afar, then lost in the crowd,
Already feel something between us but I don't really
know how.

The music softens and a change in key unlocks this
treasure of dance hauls,
Sweeping my feet around the floor and bringing them
to yours.

At a loss for words, my heart starts beating quick.
Our lines of dance have crossed, our time together
starts to tick.

Nervously I open my hand, and offer it to you.

You smile and nod.

Time...
Stands...
Still...

Our fingers touch.
There's a spark.
You feel it too.

Electricity charges through me,
Fusing our separate currents into a joint future,
But who knows what's ahead.

My eyes rise up and are met by such a beaming grin you
cause my heart to overflow
With bubbles of joy making my whole body glow.

Inching closer, swapping void with presence, our bodies
align,
Finding a feeling we've known from before,
but continue to explore,
Everything that happens as we move around the floor.

My heart pumping like a gun, I offer you the right to my
bare arms.

You enter the space and we share an embrace
so tender and close, feels... more natural than most.

Eyes closed now, only you and I in this space.
Hiding from the world in our own special place.

Pulsing together in both music and chest,
Each beat air-drops a desire we both want to express.

Questing shapes, passed between us, morph from
'yours' and 'mine' to 'ours'
Sharing our secrets in silence for what must have been
hours.

Opening my eyes, and becoming instantly lost in yours.
Words no longer needed as we share the same thoughts.

Tingles all through me as you reach up my neck and face,
Pure bliss... I could spend a lifetime in this closing embrace.

The bubble breaks, as clapping erupts across the floor,
Last track's played, but we both want more.

A curtain fall brings the sunlight of a new day.
A million heartbeats exchanged as our touch slips away.

You reach back to me and, with a squeeze, return my heart.
Looks a bit different from what it did at the start.

It hurts a little as I push it back through,
But feels better somehow, almost... fixed? Thank you.

Eyes caught in each others, we know it's not the end,
Realising we've both made a wonderful new life friend.

Happiness and love fills my body and mind,
Whilst the night's now over, our souls forever will be entwined.

Bagatelle 1

A single note plays by its own rules.
Takes as long as it wants, not moving at all,
or can tone up and scale the highest heights.

If it wants a rest, it'll happily sit outside a few bars.
Then when it's time to leave,
put the pedal down and fade off into the distance.

Bagatelle 2

It'll pick you up, put you down,
spin your whole world around,
and leave you with feelings so pleasant.

Enjoy listening alone,
with friends or unknowns
Music's gift is an ever changing present.

*bagatelle: a short unpretentious instrumental
composition*

Artists of the Forest

The Autumn artists come out at night,
Drawn by falling seeds and the birds migrating
flight.

They emerge in secret from the woodland
canopies,
To work their magic across all of the trees.

Laying their brushes gently down,
They soak up all the mottled browns

From deep within the forest floor
Then their nightly task begins once more.

Gymnasts of the trees,
They work their way up and around the leaves.

Dibbing and dabbing their shades as they go,
A kaleidoscope of colour now begins to show.

Their nightly work complete the artists sit and
admire
The beautiful creations with all the colours of fire.

With the light of a new sun, all the artists drift away,
Their new creations only lasting for a day,

As they're drawn to repeat this each and every
night,
Addicted to the patterns and the play of dark with
light.

Building layers on layers of paint on paint
Til the leaves start to fall under too much weight

As the nights grow dark and winter draws near
The artists know their job is over, at least until next
year.

This is Manchester

As you *Step On* through the Buzzing streets upon
your Northern souls,
To places where bread comes in muffins, barm
cakes and rolls.

You'll *'Never Forget'* *'This Charming Man'*'s
'Morning Glory'
As the Guardian fights for an independent story.

Uncle Joe's Balls are mint and keep your mouth
smelling fresh,
and a classic Vimto's there for a non-alcoholic
sesh.

Northern humour can be dry, which helps when it's
proper raining.
Still... the weather won't derail either team as
they're training.

Free speech at the Free Trade led to deeds not
words,
With Pankhurst from the Moss Side planting seeds,
not for the birds.

From talking bobbins over a brew, to a workers co-operative,
And Turing proving **he's** the Enigma, as the code began to give.

This is Manchester, we do things differently here
Always ready to chat and joke with new folk throughout the year.
The Gay Village is the place where we all say it with Pride,
Wherever in this world I am, I'll be a Manc inside.

That note...

That note can launch a symphony
That fills a crowd with awe,
Or introduce an encore
when the punters clap for more.

That note can start a epic gig
then be drowned in all the cheers,
Or be the time you open up
and share all your greatest fears.

That note can match a hand,
on the bus you ran for - only to miss,
Or share the moment that gorgeous date leans in
for your first kiss.

That note can share the point in time of the most
beautiful thing you've heard,
Or be on an actor's closing breath as they utter
their final word.

That note can be the point at which the tears begin
to show,
Or the second that happiness fills your face as your
smile begins to grow.

So many moments captured, thoughts, feelings all
come flooding back
like a tidal wave
As the melodies play
each linked to their own soundtrack.

Personali-tea

A mug of *English Breakfast* starts the day
with positivity.
The whistling kettle's tunes show the tea
dance's musicality.

Sit a while with a *Camomile* and transcend into
tranquility,
Or walk through nature with *Echinacea*, to escape all
the anxiety.

In her garden, *Rose* has a delicate femininity.
Jasmine though, that little tease, pops our buds with her
sensuality.

Earl Grey's airs and graces profess his Bergamot
Nobility,
Whilst *Lady Grey*, more refined, has essence of
sensibility.

So try *Assam*ple of this leaf after *Oolong* day in reality,
Or cuddle in each others *Lapsang* relax in true serenity.

A cup of *Chai* with an apple pie have a
delicious com-palatab-ility,
But it's *Lemon and Ginger*, the zingy root
bringer, that's my speciality.

Cuddle Puddle

There's an extra special time on those weekends
away,
When the hour hand draws the blinds on the end of
a day,
As the energy drops
and everyone flops
on each other and starts to nuzzle,
Slotting heads into arms,
and chests under palms,
like parts of a moving puzzle.

Sheer happiness fills us, breathing as one,
Tummies filling up with cuddles as we all feast
upon
A love that has never been so pure,
As this body of heavenly bodies,
constellating across the floor.

Snooze

Uhhhh.

Five more minutes.

The day can wait,
it's not going to mind if I'm a *teeny* bit late.

Pressing snooze,
Nothing to lose
And snuggle back into the sack

Heavy eyelids start to betray me,
As voices from dreams state start to replay
the stories and invite me back...

Uhhhhh, five minutes already?
Ahhh that went too fast...
Press it again and hope it'll last...

Ok, I'm awake, let's do this! Time to rise,
wipe the sleep from out my eyes,
start to climb out,
check the time out,
Now to fi...aahhhh sugar!, I've done it again!!
Hit the wrong button and now it's gone 10!

How many times have I done this before?
Well it stops **now**. That's it! No more!

Thinking I could get away with an extra nap,
That's the **last** time I fall into that trap!

Right. Damage limitation,
or honest reparation?
Got to play it safe or I'll get a reputation.

Think brain, what was the first thing I had to do?
Something about sending that report through...?
but, hold on...
Boss said that could wait til Monday to send,
which means it must be... the weekend.

Yesss...

What happens to our dreams?

What happens to our dreams when we
wake in the night
Are they pulled up by the moon and captured in
starlight?
Disappointed dreamers,
Try and grasp them back in vain
From the sea of broken stories lost beyond the
window pane.

What happens to the people, do they still exist?
Do they wonder where we've gone to, are we ever
missed?
What happens to the narrative if no one's in
control?
Can someone who's just drifted off pick up the
leading role
And continue on the journey to the next phase of
the story
Defeat the dragon, save the town and bathe in all
the glory.

Does it then keep passing on like that in a never ending chain?
Circling it's way around the world, before coming back again
To that initial dreamer, who's probably now forgot
The adventure and excitement of that awe inspiring plot.

So if you ever have a dream, that's been taken by the sky,
And thought it's probably gone for good, then you can always try
Picturing it around the world and if you're timing's true,
The story may pick up once more as it passes back to you,
Reigniting the wondrous tale, with all the thrills it holds,
So you can relish every moment as it once again unfolds.

Brave New Love

The question.

The question, you ask me.

The one my mind still fears,
But perversely longs to hear.
'Could we be more than friends?'

Breathe...

A 'Sliding Doors' moment we can cross, but
tracking back's an impossible journey.

To me, the answer always seemed so sure,
But waves of fear
Now lapping my brain ever more,
Eroding what once was so clear.

Pause...

I reach inside, remove the lid and layers of tissue
paper that hide and protect my vulnerable heart, to
reveal what might be left after all this time.

Still there, but just as raw as before. So delicate,
Whilst now whole again,
The cracks still remain
Showing I shouldn't risk any more pain.

How to phrase this,
In ways this will hurt you less than me...

When I said cuddles with friends are **the** best thing,
I meant every word and hoped you felt the same.
But my words never came to back up the claim
or explain why I feel the way I do.
I say, 'I love you so so much',
But there's more to it than that though, I love the
touch of so many others too.

This isn't rejection, but my reflection on a repeating
series of lives leading to the same broken heart,
With stories that start
Only to be cut short, by putting one at the centre,
and pushing others apart.

My heart's been torn so many times in multiple
directions, perceived expectations confusing me
into silence.
Scared of the damage I'll cause
with this double edged sword
because my truth isn't "normal".

Breathe...

Lines prepared, I'm ready to go but know I'd rather
rewind to a time when "just friends" was all there
was.

"Just friends" **isn't** second best though, the rest
don't yet know just how good "just" can be. Justice
for "just" is what we need.

An emotional lake behind the dam of my eyes,
fighting the urge to cry,
Sees me hoping this isn't the sunset time for our
hearts,
But the dawn of greater than the sum of our parts.

Love you truly,
A next level friendship sails through me,
A little hugboat as you say you don't **just**
understand, but feel the same way too!
Glory phew!

Relax...

Worries now sinking,
You take my hand and sync in
with the feelings we've aired.
The connection we shared
almost dropped, but you dialed it back up, clicked
restore,
Now stronger than before
As we enter this brave new love unleashed for us
all.

Rainbows

A rainbow spans more distance than we'll ever
understand
Like the love between two friends set apart by sea
and land.
Sitting beneath the same great sky, we'll never be
alone,
With rainbows to remind us of the happiness we've
known.

So come and shelter with me and step in from all
life's rain,
Let's both stay safe and cozy til the sun shines
once again.
Things **will** return to normal once the current storm
is through,
When joyous bands of coloured light bring hope
back into view.

And if you find you're struggling, no matter what
you try,
I'll push out love and kindness in an arc across the
sky.
I'll send so many rainbows and be here to help you
through,
Each one filled with love and hugs beaming out
from me to you.

The Ant and The Tree

'How tall must you be?'
Said the ant to the tree
As she slowly climbed up his bark
'Thought I'd take in the view
But when I get to
The top, it'll probably be dark'.

Said the tree to the ant
'I'm just a small plant
That's grown over time to this size.
You'll make it I know,
But if you're too slow
Stay on me and see the sunrise'.

Pushing down with her toes
Up the tree trunk she rose
Til she finally got to the summit.
What a view to behold
As the great tree told
Her 'I knew, and was sure you could do it'.

So far up from the floor
The ant loved all she saw
And the tree shared all that he knew.
They chatted for hours
Naming all of the flowers
They could see, till they went out of view.

As time passed away
Through the rest of the day
The ant said 'I must finally go'.
The tree said 'Please,
Take one a my leaves
And glide down, much easier I know'.

Said the ant, 'You're a gem'
As she walked up the stem
'I'd love to come back again please.
I've really loved talking,
And that leaf saves me walking
And looks after my ant colo-knees'.

So each week she returns
And they share what they learn
About everything on land they can see.
'I'm so glad I first came,'
The ant starts to exclaim
Says the tree, 'I'm so happy you climbed me'.

Underground Love

It was getting *Leyton* and I'd been standing waiting
too long for my date to show.
Feet sore, didn't want to *Stanmore*, so they became
someone I *Euston*-know

Cutting my loss didn't want to *Brent Cross*, I
glanced across and that's when I saw her drop it.

She bent down to her *Neasden* her toes, looked
embarrassed, before she rose,
as she couldn't lift it from that pose.

On instinct, I went to *Alperton* it over.

The heavy scooter, which felt it must've weighed
more than an *Oak Wood*'ve, finally shifted and she
lifted her face, revealing such beautiful *Bethnal
Green* eyes and a wonderful hairstyle far nicer than
my *Barbican* ever make mine.

I complemented *High Barnett*
and asked how she kept it in her helmet,

She giggled, the kind of laugh that can make the
South and *Northholt* for just a second.

After saying which way I was going,
the thing I thought would be most reassuring,
she smiled and said she's goin' that way *Too(ting)*

I introduced myself;

'*Colindale* pleased to meet you',
'I'm *Victoria*' she blushed 'pleased to meet you too'

We laughed and joked so much on that short walk,
Moredan I've ever laughed with anyone after such
small talk.

Words rushing through my head,
when we got to my tube stop I said,
I'm not a *Richmond*on't live on a *Goodge Street*,
but if you like me... I'd love to re-meet.
"Remeet?" She asked "Is that *Monument* to say?"
My turn to blush,
from this little crush,
I said 'I'd love to see you another day'.

So that was our meet cute,
sweeter than any *Baker Street*
And started off this Circle loop
of, Sleep, Love Life repeat

The Time Traveller's Dilemma

(Care Warning: Loss of a loved one)

You
Will destroy
It
This task you've set yourself
I'm telling you
You can do this
Ignore those that say
Time travel ultimately brings sadness
The many wonders and experiences of the world
mean nothing compared to her

What makes you expect
You can make equally wonderful new memories
with friends

That fateful night was the end of it all
You shouldn't believe
It's not worth the effort
If you do the research, you can go back and save
her
It'd be foolish to think
It's a waste of time
For a few years

Your friends will still wait for you when you don't
stay in touch
Why would you think
Your friends will drift away
Over time
You hide away and say no to every offer
When friends invite you out
For a different reason every time
It never works
No matter what
You just can't
Whilst saving her is the only thing you want
You
Will defeat
The paradox
Travel back to save her
Do not
Think anymore of it

*A bolt of energy shakes the room and a person
appears in the smoke from the far side, a desperate
expression on their face. You do a double take, it's
like looking in a mirror, except this version of you
looks so much older. They waste no time, and start
their urgent warning.*

'You can't save her, it's useless. Promise me you
won't...'

*Time starts to re-wind, reversing what's just
happened, as you now read the poem backwards...*

Mystery at the Lake House

Our story begins in October last year,
a young group of friends with nothing to fear
book a house by the lake for a week or so,
pack up all their things and off they go.

On arriving, the place feels cold and dark,
and gives them shivers as they drive up to park.
The wooden steps creek as they open the door,
turning the latch they enter as four.

The main room brings a sense of unease,
paintings hung off axis and a windless breeze
seems to flow through the room and rattle the
chairs,
before changing direction and heading upstairs.

They follow the gust and as they ascend,
they hear a murmur that sounds like 'friennnnnnd'
This shakes them a little and they look round in
vain,
each desperate for one of them to explain.

The lad at the front steps onto the landing,
the lights flicker then burst which scares them to
standing.

Tiptoeing across to the first room they see,
one of them turns back, too scared, leaving only
three.

Pushing gently on the old wooden door,
they enter in silence and see sat on the floor
a ghostly child pushing cars around a track,
Causing another to scream and turn back.

Now two remain to face this child who's started to
rise,
cowering in the corner the youngsters fall to half
their size.
The child reaches out a hand, it's withered fingers
half gone
A retreating scream from the other, means we're
now down to one.

Just this brave soul remains now, too scared to run
'Please don't hurt me, I'm a friend, let's play and
have some fun'
At this the child stops and smiles a warmth passing
over its face.
It sits and points down at the cars, looks up and
asks 'race?'

Having a brother of his own, the brave youngster
understands
Sitting down next to the kid he smiles and opens
his hands.

With delight the ghost finds a car and happily squeals
and passes him a racer with a shiny set of wheels.

'Go' shouts the child, and around the track they zoom,
weaving around each other as they lurch about the room
The youngster tries in vain to keep up with the speedy kid
But remembers how nice it felt to let his brother win
- which he always did

The youngster pretends to lose control and drive straight through both the ponds.
The kid giggles and they start to form the unlikeliest of bonds
Round and round they continue to race,
but who's going to end up in first place?

'Nice move!' the youngster commentates, the kid swerving the final bend
Then as they cross the finish line the kid looks up and asks 'friend?'
The look of joy on this ghost's face make it an instant 'yes'
The kid runs around the room with glee, making such a mess.

And with that a beam of light appears from the far side wall
The kid looks up startled, not getting it at all.
Then a look of understanding, that they've now reached their peace
And can at last cross over and the pain can finally cease

'Thank you' says the kid as they start to walk across
The stunned youngster sits in silence, words are at a loss
Waving their hand, the little kid starts to step on through.
'Goodbye' the youngster calls out and begins to wave back too

The portal of light envelops the child as they slowly disappear
The youngster's heartstrings start to pull as he wipes away a tear.
So little time together but the connection felt so real
Who would have thought that these two would ever start to feel
such a sense of friendship based on just a toy car ride
That allowed the kid to gain peace and pass on to the other side.

I love you NBD

(inspired by Carsie Blanton's blog)

I love you.

But it's no big deal.

I'm not expecting you to love me back,
It's just hearing your voice, makes my heart shift
track
And jump like a kid with nothing to fear,
You block out all the noise, and remind me why I'm
here.

I love you.

But it's no big deal,

When we're about to hang up my heart wags its tail
like a puppy desperate to walk,
in anticipation of the next time that we'll talk .

I love you.

But it's no big deal, I love others too.

Though there's no competition for which
disposition, I like best
Cos I love what's **different** between you and the
rest,
And I love them all for the same reason too,
What makes them *them* and makes you *you*.

I love you.

But it's no big deal.

I don't want to settle and I'm not trying to get in your
pants,
I want to be independent **with** you, not making life
plans.
Live our own separate lives, not do chores on
repeat,
and have moments of magic whenever we meet.

Let the joy that we share
Have unending growth
And for you, I'll be there,
Til time catches us both.

But it's no big deal,

I just love you.

Acknowledgments

To my family for a lifetime of love and support through everything.

To my friends for bringing so much joy.

To the special group of friends from Poetrytime, Storytime and the Catch up Crew, who have been a constant beam of light through a very dark year.

And finally, an extra special thank you to Frankie, who's love of words and boundless energy to share stories sparked these groups, and without whom, none of this collection would have ever been written.

Big hugs.

Printed in Poland
by Amazon Fulfillment
Poland Sp. z o.o., Wrocław